For Leo and his family, and the entire INAD community. Never lose hope.

When a child gets hurt, a typical response might be "kiss it to make it feel better." This method works in most cases; however, for Leo it's not so simple.

Bisous for Leo was written for a young boy, Leo, who has a very rare, genetic, neurodegenerative disease called INAD - Infantile Neuroaxonal Dystrophy, or in simpler terms, "Parkinson's mixed with Alzheimer's for kids." Born in France to a Parisian father and an American mother, the energetic boy developed like a typical child well into his first year, when his parents noticed a developmental regression. After much testing, the diagnosis was rendered.

The disease usually develops between 6 months and 3 years of age. Children affected will lose all acquired skills including mental and cognitive abilities, as seen in Alzheimer's, and physical abilities, as seen in Parkinson's, resulting in death likely before they reach their 10th birthday.

In November 2018, 6 months after Leo was diagnosed, he was enrolled as the first INAD patient in the very first clinical trial. There are currently no other known treatments. This is the only chance at hopefully stopping or, at the very least, slowing down the progression of the disease until a cure is available. Gene Therapy, which has cured other rare diseases, would be the only way to possibly save his life. Leo's parents are hoping that trials will start before the end of the year because he doesn't have a lot of time. Leo no longer walks or talks and he is regressing rapidly. He doesn't give up and neither do his parents in their search for saving their son's life.

INAD is considered a neurodegenerative disease. Neurodegenerative diseases affect millions of people worldwide. Alzheimer's disease and Parkinson's disease are the most common types, with more than 44 million living with Alzheimer's disease or a related dementia, and an estimated 7-10 million living with Parkinson's disease. Finding a cure for the infant forms of the diseases could lead the way to finding better treatments and ultimately a cure for the adult versions. Treating patients as early as possible have been shown to be more beneficial, of course, than after they have lost acquired skills. This is why working quickly to find the cure is key.

HELP US KISS INAD GOODBYE

In September 2018, Bisous For Leo launched an Instagram account @BisousForLeo encouraging its followers to help kiss INAD goodbye, not just for Leo but for all children affected by the disease. People from all around the world have been posting their kisses (or Bisous as they say in French) and tagging Bisous For Leo to help raise awareness. The campaign also raises funds to benefit the INADcure Foundation (www.inadcure.org), the only U.S.-based non-profit dedicated to the INAD community. The INADcure Foundation works to identify and fund the most promising INAD research projects. All of the proceeds raised from this book will go directly to the INADcure Foundation and hopefully help eradicate this devastating disease.

Please post your own bisous and donate at BisousForLeo.org so we can help save his life.

Designed by Leo's mom

BISOUS FOR LEO

by Whitney Patapoff

Illustrated by Pauline Vuarin

ISBN: 978-1-7332070-0-3 (English Book)
ISBN: 978-1-7332070-1-0 (English eBook)
ISBN: 978-1-7332070-2-7 (French Book)
ISBN: 978-1-7332070-3-4 (French eBook)

Hello, my name is Leo and I'm two years old.
I'm brave, smart, dashing, and bold!

I come from a small pond in France.
I love to fly, swim, and dance!

When I fall down and skin my knee,
a kiss from Mom and Dad is all I need.

The more kisses they give, the better I feel.
Imagine if kisses were all we needed to heal.

It turns out I have a boo-boo that you can't see,
and there are many other ducks in the world like me.

If kisses make me feel better, it must be the same for them.
So I'll make it my mission to collect kisses for my friends!

I'll fly anywhere, over land and sea.
I may be little, but I'm brave as can be.

No matter how fast or how tall,
I'm not afraid of any other animal.

I'll tell them my story and hope that they listen.
When we work together, we can accomplish any mission!

Even if it gets dark or a little scary,
I'll gather as many kisses as I can carry.

Help me fill my bag with BISOUS as I go.
That's KISSES in French, in case you didn't know!

Bisous from a FROG
Bisous from a COW
Count the bisous if you know how!

Bisous from a SNAKE
Bisous from a BUNNY

Gee, their soft, little noses
feel funny.

Bisous from a LION
Bisous from a GIRAFFE
Oh, how their long tongues make me laugh!

Bisous from a RHINO
Bisous from a DOVE
Wow, I sure do feel the love!

Bisous from an ELEPHANT
Bisous from a PIG
My bag is getting so full and big!

Bisous from a DOLPHIN
Bisous from a SHARK
The sun is setting, it's starting to get dark.

Bisous from a CHICKEN
Bisous from a SHEEP
I'm getting very tired and need to get some sleep.

Before I go, I'm sending bisous back,
to all of the animals that give a quack!

Thank you for your love and generosity;
it means so much to my family and me.

Now I will lay down for the night to rest,
all snuggled up in my cozy nest.
As I sleep, I'll dream the same dream I have each night,
that these BISOUS reach my friends
and help make everything alright.
Then in the morning, when I wake with glee,
I'll gather more BISOUS for my friends and me!

Whitney Patapoff

was inspired by Leo's story and immense courage. She lives in Chicago, IL with her husband Richard and two boys, Mason and Wesley. This is her first book.

Pauline Vuarin

is an artist and also Leo's aunt. She lives in the south of France with her husband Antonio and son Ernesto. This is also her first book.

Please visit
www.BisousForLeo.org
for more information, to donate, and to
HELP US KISS INAD GOODBYE